LEVEL FOUR Chapters

Ripley Readers

All true and unbelievable!

Learning to read. Reading to learn!

LEVEL ONE Sounding It Out Preschool-Kindergarten
For kids who know their alphabet and are starting to sound out words.

learning sight words • beginning reading • sounding out words

LEVEL TWO Reading with Help Preschool-Grade 1
For kids who know sight words and are learning to sound out new words.

expanding vocabulary • building confidence • sounding out bigger words

LEVEL THREE Independent Reading Grades 1-3
For kids who are beginning to read on their own.

introducing paragraphs • challenging vocabulary • reading for comprehension

LEVEL FOUR Chapters Grades 2-4
For confident readers who enjoy a mixture of images and story.

reading for learning • more complex content • feeding curiosity

Ripley Readers Designed to help kids build their reading skills and confidence at any level, this program offers a variety of fun, entertaining, and unbelievable topics to interest even the most reluctant readers. With stories and information that will spark their curiosity, each book will motivate them to start and keep reading.

Vice President, Licensing & Publishing Amanda Joiner
Editorial Manager Carrie Bolin

Editor Jessica Firpi
Writer Korynn Wible-Freels
Designer Scott Swanson
Reprographics Bob Prohaska
Production Design Luis Fuentes
Proofreader Rachel Paul

Published by Ripley Publishing 2021

10 9 8 7 6 5 4 3 2 1

Copyright © 2021 Ripley Publishing

ISBN: 978-1-60991-409-7

No part of this publication may be reproduced in whole or in part, stored in a retrieval system, or transmitted in any form by any means, electronic, mechanical, photocopying, recording, or otherwise, without written permission from the publisher.

For more information regarding permission, contact:
VP Licensing & Publishing
Ripley Entertainment Inc.
7576 Kingspointe Parkway, Suite 188
Orlando, Florida 32819

Email: publishing@ripleys.com
www.ripleys.com/books
Manufactured in China in May 2020.

First Printing

Library of Congress Control Number: 2020937145

PUBLISHER'S NOTE
While every effort has been made to verify the accuracy of the entries in this book, the Publisher cannot be held responsible for any errors contained in the work. They would be glad to receive any information from readers.

PHOTO CREDITS

8 (br) Kurt Miller/Stocktrek Images/Getty Images, **10** Granamour Weems Collection/Alamy Stock Photo, **13** (tr) Frederic Lewis/Hulton Archive/Getty Images, **24** Culture Club/Getty Images, **25** (t) ZU_09/Getty Images, **27** ZU_09/Getty Images, **30** Public Domain {{PD-US}} Friedrich Johann Justin Bertuch (1747-1822), **31** Public Domain {{PD-US}} Wenceslaus Hollar (1607-1677), **36** (t) Imagno/Getty Images, **42** (t) RichVintage/Getty Images, (cr) Created by Scott Swanson, **Master Graphics** Created by Scott Swanson

Key: t = top, b = bottom, c = center, l = left, r = right

All other photos are from Shutterstock or Ripley Entertainment Inc. Every attempt has been made to acknowledge correctly and contact copyright holders and we apologize in advance for any unintentional errors or omissions, which will be corrected in future editions.

LEXILE®, LEXILE FRAMEWORK®, LEXILE ANALYZER®, the LEXILE® logo and POWERV® are trademarks of MetaMetrics, Inc., and are registered in the United States and abroad. The trademarks and names of other companies and products mentioned herein are the property of their respective owners. Copyright © 2020 MetaMetrics, Inc. All rights reserved.

Ripley Readers

Mythical Creatures!

All true and unbelievable!

Ripley
PUBLISHING

a Jim Pattison Company

TABLE OF CONTENTS

Chapter 1
Where Do They Come From? ...6

Chapter 2
Pop-Culture Creatures............ 10

Chapter 3
It's All Greek to Me 18

Chapter 4
Mythic Mayhem! 26

Chapter 5
Around the World.................... 34

Chapter 6
Cryptic Creatures 40

Glossary 46

CHAPTER 1
WHERE DO THEY COME FROM?

If there is one thing that can stand the test of time, it is the tale of a **mythical** creature. From fairies to monsters of the deep, some creatures bring fortune and others bring fear.

Long ago, ancient cultures needed a way to understand the world around them. Many **legends** started as a way to explain strange events, like digging up giant bones or spotting a weird animal out at sea.

CHAPTER 2
POP-CULTURE CREATURES

Books, movies, and TV have so many mythical creatures. Let's sink "tooth and nail" into learning about these beings!

WEREWOLF

A werewolf is a human who transforms into a wolf or a mix of human and wolf. Depending on the culture, this could be caused by a curse or with the help of a magical object. Werewolf stories were told as far back as the Bronze Age (3000 to 1200 B.C.). They were popular in France during the 1400s and 1500s. Some people even claimed to see a werewolf change with their own eyes! How they lived to tell the tale remains a mystery…

VAMPIRE

A vampire is an **immortal** man or woman who drinks human blood. Legend has it that vampires can be killed by sunlight, a wooden stake, garlic, or by cutting off their heads.

Some believe that rabies, a deadly disease that causes madness, is to blame. People with rabies experienced a fear of water and even had **insomnia**, which might have led people to believe that vampires did not drink water and were creatures of the night.

UNICORN

Unlike other creepy beasts, the unicorn is a beautiful mythical creature. Many cultures believe the unicorn has healing powers, but good luck catching one! These pure-white ponies are quick. It is assumed that one-horned Indian rhinos were mistaken for unicorns. It's not exactly the graceful creature we see in books and movies!

DRAGON

Nearly every ancient culture in the world has a story about dragons. Some describe them as long, scaly serpents, others as fire-breathing brutes. Many believe that dinosaur bones were behind the dragon legends. Others even wonder if a few of these ancient reptiles lingered just long enough for mankind to see them. Could it be possible? We may never know!

Believe It or Not! The study of dinosaurs is still pretty new. The word *dinosaur* wasn't even invented until 1842!

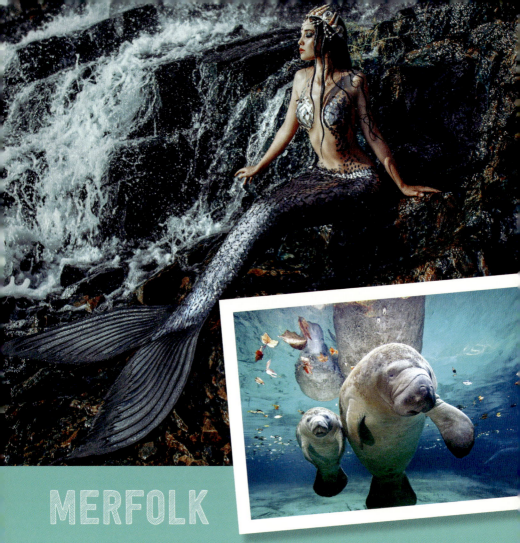

MERFOLK

Mythical merfolk are unlike the mermaids in movies! Merfolk were thought to be bad luck to sailors, and seeing one meant disaster. Mermaids were also known to lure men into unsafe waters with their beautiful singing. The inspiration for merfolk legends? Manatees!

FAIRY

Did you know that the very first fairies were not tiny? They didn't even have wings! The word *fairy* is from the Middle Ages. Many cultures have a version of a fairy. Some legends describe fairies as kind and magical, while others say they are cruel and even dangerous tricksters! Which do you believe?

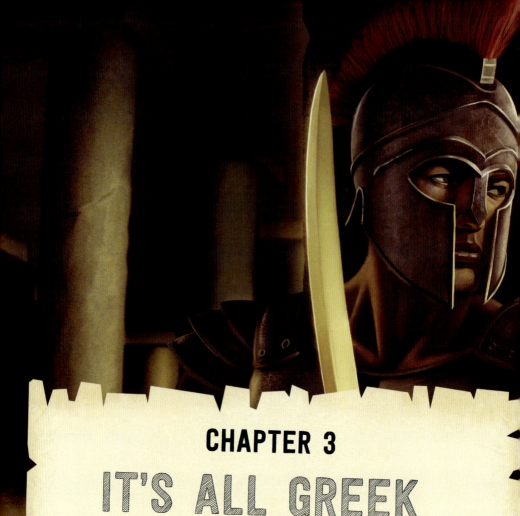

CHAPTER 3
IT'S ALL GREEK TO ME

Greece has always been known for its mythology. Two **epics** called *The Iliad* and *The Odyssey* give us a better look at some of ancient Greece's most popular fabled creatures!

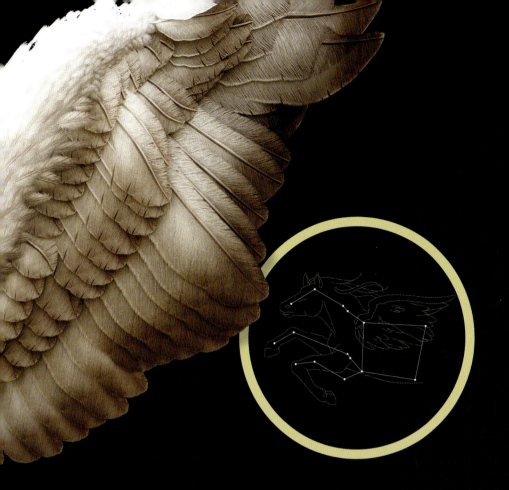

Pegasus is a winged horse born from Medusa's blood when she was beheaded. (Medusa is a Greek mythical creature, too. She is a woman who was cursed with snakes for hair.) It is said that Pegasus is now a servant of the god Zeus on Mount Olympus.

You can even look to the night sky and see a **constellation** of Pegasus!

    A centaur is a creature with the top half of a human and the bottom half of a horse. Legend says that when the god Zeus noticed a man named Ixion admiring Hera (Zeus's wife), Zeus designed a look-alike of her out of clouds. Ixion and the look-alike Hera gave birth to the centaur race. Hunters on horseback are thought to have inspired the combat-loving centaurs.

A siren is a creature with the head and body of a woman and the wings of a bird. Sirens are said to be the daughters of either the sea god Phorcys (*FOR-sis*) or the river god Achelous (*Ack-eh-LOW-us*). Like mermaids, sirens are known for luring sailors to their deaths with their enchanting voices.

CHAPTER 4
MYTHIC MAYHEM!

When it comes to mischief, there are some creatures that have a talent for trouble! See if you recognize any of these mythical pests!

Ancient trolls were bumpy, grumpy creatures who lived in the mountains or underground caves. In a legend from Iceland, one evil Christmas troll named Grýla was even said to kidnap naughty children and eat them!

Have you heard of the basilisk? A giant serpent with toxic breath, the basilisk can even kill just by looking a person in the eye. In fact, basilisk hunters would carry mirrors, hoping the basilisk would see its own deadly stare. During the Middle Ages, the basilisk was said to have the head of a rooster and wings of a bat.

The ocean may seem calm, but sailors say a deadly monster dwells beneath the surface. With the tentacles of a massive squid, the kraken is said to have dragged entire ships down to the ocean floor. It can even cause a whirlpool just by diving underwater!

Believe It or Not! The kraken is based off a real creature—the giant squid! A rare sight, giant squid have been known to grow 33 feet long on average. That is longer than a school bus!

CHAPTER 5
AROUND THE WORLD

CREATURE: Genies (or Jinnis)

ORIGIN: Arabic

DESCRIPTION: supernatural creatures more powerful than humans but less mighty than angels or demons

KNOWN FOR: taking on human or animal form, inspiring poets and **fortune-tellers**, and tormenting people who have wronged them

CREATURE: Sphinx (*s-FINK-s*)

ORIGIN: Greek and Egyptian

DESCRIPTION: head of a human, body of a lion

KNOWN FOR: wisdom and clever riddles

CREATURE: Krampus

ORIGIN: European

DESCRIPTION: top half demon, bottom half goat

KNOWN FOR: appearing in the homes of naughty children and punishing them with sticks during Christmas

CREATURE: Yeti

ORIGIN: Himalayan

DESCRIPTION: a furry ape-like creature

KNOWN FOR: secretly dwelling in the Himalayan mountains, leaving behind giant footprints

CREATURE: Gnome (*NOAM*)

ORIGIN: European

DESCRIPTION: small spirits who resemble old men and live underground

KNOWN FOR: guarding hidden treasures in the earth

CREATURE: Kitsune (*keet-soo-NAY*)

ORIGIN: Japanese

DESCRIPTION: godlike foxes that can change into humans

KNOWN FOR: wisdom, protection, and mischief

CHAPTER 5
CRYPTIC CREATURES

No creatures fit Ripley's slogan better than the **cryptids**. Are they real? You can choose to believe it or not! **Cryptozoology** is the study of creatures that may or may not exist.

BIGFOOT

If you live in North America, chances are you have heard of Bigfoot. Many believe this ape-man creature roams the forest. But no actual trace of Bigfoot has ever been found!

Believe It or Not! It is illegal to kill Bigfoot in the state of Washington!

LOCH NESS MONSTER

Scientists say that dinosaurs went **extinct** millions of years ago. Yet some people in Scotland think otherwise! The Loch Ness Monster is often thought to be a **plesiosaur**. At an amazing 745 feet deep, Loch Ness could certainly hide a giant creature, or at least keep us wondering about it!

Plesiosaur

CHUPACABRA

One of the newest mythical creatures is the Chupacabra. This foxlike creature is said to have spikes along its back and a thirst for goat blood! The Chupacabra was first reported in Puerto Rico in 1995. Stories of it have been around since the 1970s. It has since been revealed to be a sick, hairless raccoon.

Though many of these famous fables have some kind of explanation, one thing is for sure: seeing isn't always believing. Sometimes, believing is seeing!

Glossary

constellation: a group of stars that might look like a person or thing.

cryptid: an animal that has not been proven to exist.

cryptozoology: the study of and search for legendary animals.

epic: a long poem about a legendary event or hero.

extinct: something that no longer exists.

fortune-teller: a person who claims to predict the future.

immortal: to live forever.

insomnia: the inability to get enough sleep or fall asleep.

legend: a historical story that cannot be proven.

mythical: a person or thing that is imaginary, false, or cannot be proven.

plesiosaur: a marine reptile with flippers from the Mesozoic era.

whirlpool: water that moves quickly in a circle and can force objects down its center.

Ripley Readers

All true and unbelievable!

Ready for More?

Ripley Readers feature unbelievable but true facts and stories!

 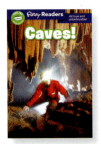 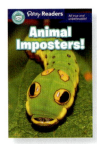 

   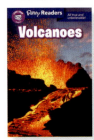

For more information about Ripley's Believe It or Not!, go to www.ripleys.com